Who's *in Your* ROOM?

THE SECRET TO CREATING YOUR BEST LIFE

Who's
in Your
ROOM?

THE SECRET TO CREATING YOUR BEST LIFE

Ivan Misner, Ph.D. Stewart Emery, L.H.D. Rick Sapio

Indigo River Publishing

Editors: Jackson Haynes and Regina Cornell
Book Design: mycustombookcover.com

Indigo River Publishing
3 West Garden Street, Ste. 352
Pensacola, FL 32502
www.indigoriverpublishing.com

Ordering Information:
Quantity sales: Special discounts are available on quantity purchases by corporations, associations, and others. For details, contact the publisher at the address above.

Orders by US trade bookstores and wholesalers: Please contact the publisher at the address above.

Printed in the United States of America

Library of Congress Control Number: 2018959468
Soft Cover ISBN: 978-1-948080-46-0
Hard Cover ISBN: 978-1-948080-47-7

First Edition

With Indigo River Publishing, you can always expect great books, strong voices, and meaningful messages. Most importantly, you'll always find...words worth reading.

TABLE OF CONTENTS

Imagine You Live in One Room 1

Guarding Your Door.. 9

Determining Your Values 15

Assessing Who's in Your Room 33

Training Your Doorman...41

Handling People Already in Your Room...........................53

Living in Your Room 65

The Room You Design 75

Chapter One

Imagine You Live in One Room

Imagine that you live in one room. Imagine that you live your entire life in this room where you and your imagination create your life. Anything at all can be contained in this space. Inside are all the people who enter, as well as the relationships and obligations that come with them. You can update and expand your room to accommodate new possibilities in your life. However, there is a unique and permanent feature of this room: it only has one door. It will only ever have one door. You may think that there is nothing unique or unusual about this one-door thing. Lots of rooms only have one door. True, but this particular door is a one-way door. "Enter Only." NO EXIT. Whoever comes through this door, and whatever they bring with them, cannot leave—ever. They will be with you in your room for the rest of your life.

This concept matters to you because the quality of your life depends upon who's in your room.

One more time: *The quality of your life depends upon who's in your room.*

It does. The person you become and whether or not you are happy and successful depends on who's in your room. Really.

Hit pause. Time to think. How is this landing?

So who's in your room? Take a moment. Look around. Take a quick inventory. You could start with your contact list, your social media list, and check who's in your checkbook. Who's in, up close and personal? Who else is in—friends, family members, people you work with, people you love having in your room along with people you wish weren't there?

Okay. That's a moment. You'll look longer later.

Now ask yourself, based upon what you've seen so far: Would you have made different choices had you known that anybody who came into your room was going to be in it forever? Almost everyone we've asked has said yes to this question.

Now that you recognize this point, the important question going forward is this: **How are you going to select people you wish to have in your room now that you know they can never leave?**

Many people report that they immediately have an *OMG!* moment when first introduced to this notion. Some launch into flashback mode and say that for them it is like watching a high-speed rerun of their entire life. A train wreck for some, or just a very bumpy ride for others.

Now, if you are about to push back with "It can't literally be true that once people get in my room they are in it forever," instead ask yourself this: Would I be willing, from this moment on, to live as though it *were* true? In fact, neurologists report that as far as your brain is concerned, this really is true. According to renowned psychiatrist and neuroscientist Dr. Daniel Amen, founder of the Amen Clinics, "Any significant input that is received in your brain triggers neural activity that cannot simply be erased or deleted as though it never happened."

If someone hurts you, was mean to you, or belittles you, they stay in your room and they're all over your brain. Their voice is in the voice-recognition part of your brain, their face is in the facial-recognition part of your brain, and they don't go away. When you meet someone and they get anchored, they don't go away. *People may be out of your life, but they're still in your head.* The things they say and do affect your thinking, behavior, and experience—forever.

You might, for example, believe you have ended a relationship, terminated a project, or let a previous commitment go, but these events have left an indelible mark—affecting your future experience in myriad ways—for better or worse, whether you like it or not.

This realization is one of those good news/bad news deals because, to our good fortune, this is also the case when someone genuinely loves you, praises you, or skillfully mentors you.

Your past is archived in your psyche, just as your future will also be when it unfolds to become a part of your past. What's done is done. The events of the past cannot be undone. An action taken has been taken. A word uttered cannot be taken back.

We are who we are because of and in spite of others. What *can* be done is to curate your room to build a better future. Moving forward, you can very carefully choose who and what comes into your room and into your life. Choose well, and you will love your life. Don't choose well, and . . . you know how that goes! However, the good news is that later in this book we'll show you how to make better choices that will dramatically improve your life.

This mindset is all about looking forward to the future. It's not about looking back in anguish to the past. This book works from this moment forward. You will begin to treat constraining elements from your past with a new understanding of how to relate to people in the future.

Let's unpack all this a little more, starting with the here and now.

Putting the transformative power of "who's in your room?" to work begins with an inquiry rather than a rush to action.

Imagine that your life is chaotic, and let's say you want to change that. But is chaos a cause or an effect? In other words, does chaos name the disease or is it merely a symptom? *Disease* may seem too strong a word. However, when you remember that *disease* derives from the *absence of ease*, then it surely applies to this state of affairs.

Notice if there are characters in your room who gained entry carrying the curse of chaos with them. You know who we're talking about—people who don't feel they are alive unless they're immersed in drama. You might even have become one of them. The chaotic life has you living in an overcrowded room. Too many people, too much stuff, too little time.

As you continue your review of how your daily experience is being shaped by the people in your room, we're going to ask you to engage your imagination and play along a little—maybe more than a little.

So imagine that your life feels harsh and angry—perhaps not all the time, but sometimes. Now recall a specific time when you experienced harshness and anger. Put yourself back in that moment. Who's in your room with you? Notice if you have a harsh and angry person in your presence—perhaps several harsh and angry people, maybe even a mob.

On the other hand, imagine your life is filled with love and kindness. Now recall a time when your experience felt like a flood of love and kindness swirling around you and washing over you, and your room was filled with light. Notice who's in your room with you.

Dissonance and resonance are shaping your experience in each of these examples.

In physics, resonance is a phenomenon that occurs when a vibrating system or external force drives another system to oscillate at a specific preferential frequency. Imagine two pianos side by side in a room. If you hit the middle *C* key on one piano while someone presses the sustain pedal on the other one, the middle *C* string will vibrate on the second piano *without any physical action taken upon it*. This is resonance at work.

An example of dissonance almost all of us have experienced is the harsh, disagreeable sound a piece of chalk can make when moving across a chalkboard, or our feelings when we become subjected to inconsistencies between a person's actions and his or her stated values. By way of another example, most of us have experienced being hurt by the behavior of a person who professes to love us.

We human beings are like those piano strings. Some of us are even described as being high-strung. We're talking about resonance and dissonance. Resonance is an agreeable sensation, but dissonance is not. You've heard of someone's buttons being pushed; that would be a moment of dissonance. You have had this experience yourself. You have probably let it be known that certain people and situations push your buttons and get you going.

Well, it's not your buttons being pushed, not exactly; it's your strings—sometimes intensely. Sometimes this feels good (resonance) and sometimes not so much (dissonance).

The point here is that you are, metaphorically speaking, a multi-stringed work of art in progress. Who's in your room has everything to do with the emotional, intellectual, physical, and spiritual strings resonating within you. You will probably express many of these vibrations externally, such as when you see someone you love, you light up and welcome them warmly. On the other hand, if you see a person you don't care for or don't trust, you are likely to avoid them and the unpleasant inner experience of dissonance.

Sometimes we are unaware of the internal experience that is a trigger for our behavior. This is particularly the case when we become suddenly angry. It can happen abruptly, and we are in reaction mode before being conscious of what the trigger was or that our strings have been played. What can be unconscious to us can be blindingly obvious to other people, which can be a catalyst for all kinds of grief. Developing self-awareness can help significantly. You can become skilled at identifying the inner experiences of resonance and dissonance, and then consciously choose how to behave in any given moment.

If you take the time to contemplate your life, you will notice themes as you identify the relationships you have with the people in your room and all the obligations that came in with them. Allow yourself to become aware of how all of it impacts you and your daily experience of being alive. This process is not about establishing blame or fault—doing so serves no useful purpose. This process is about noticing resonance and dissonance as a guide to where you will invest more time and how you will manage your room.

Did you know that the number one regret people have when death is closing in on them is *"I wish I'd had the courage to live a life true to myself, not the life others expected of me"*? We now know this to be so from the work of Bronnie Ware, a hospice nurse who asked her patients about their regrets. Why do so many people come to the end of their lives carrying this regret?

Howard Thurman counseled, "Don't ask what the world needs. Ask what makes you come alive, and go do it. Because what the world needs are people who have come alive."

You are the architect of your emotional, mental, spiritual, and physical room. You need to craft an environment filled with resonance rather than dissonance. Build a room that makes you come alive, because . . .

The room always wins.

Chapter Two

GUARDING YOUR DOOR

Picture your room in your mind. It holds all the people you've ever let into your room—ever. That makes it pretty large. You can decorate it any way you want—but it's big, almost like an auditorium. There are people close to you whom you see regularly and know well. They are friends and family, your immediate colleagues, and others who have a significant role in your daily life. There are others behind them that you talk to occasionally. They are the people you interact with from time to time, with whom you are mostly friends or possibly indifferent about. There are others, perhaps hundreds, behind them fading off into the room who are less important in your life.

And way in the back, in hidden corners in the darkest reaches, are people you haven't thought about in years or would just as soon forget—or, perhaps, would like to bring out of the shadows once more.

Let's Consider the Door

There it sits, closed but not locked, ready to swing open when the next person pushes his or her way in. When you're very young, you can only sit and marvel at the parade of people who come through it into your room. It takes a few years before you begin to understand that not all of the people who come in are people you necessarily want in the room.

Even after you figure out the meaning and function of that door, you have to spend some time learning how and when and why you should use it. Until you reach that stage in your life, the door swings wide at the slightest touch.

You begin to wonder if there is a way to control who comes through the door. We are here to tell you that there is. You can, in fact, take control over when that door opens and when it stays shut.

You can post a bouncer.

That's right, a bouncer. Your room is like an auditorium, right? But there's only one door, and anybody who comes in can't leave. (Don't worry about the fire codes; we paid off the fire marshal in this room.) And like any good auditorium owner, you can post a bouncer who will grant entry to only those people you want in. Not on the list? Take a hike.

You know, *bouncer* sounds a bit too confrontational, doesn't it? Maybe we shouldn't call him or her a bouncer, but something less hostile. *Guard*, maybe. Even better: *Doorman*. Like the doorman in front of an apartment building or hotel. Someone who restricts entry, but in a friendly, helpful way. You can call this person a doorperson, if you prefer. We'll stick with *Doorman*, but *doorperson* works, too, as does *bouncer* or *guardian*, if you'd like. The idea of someone screening entrance to your room is much more important than the name you call that person.

Okay, we're not really talking about actually hiring a person to stand by you and guard the door to your room. We're talking about a metaphorical doorman—your conscious and subconscious mind. A process of thought and feelings to help you determine whether your door should remain closed or be opened to allow someone entry into your life.

What defines the kind of person you want your Doorman to let into your room? Success? Perhaps, but you need to know what kind of success is important to you. Is it material success? Success in personal relationships? Success in creating value for others without thinking of one's own self? Or is success simply achieving personal happiness? What is the meaning of happiness? Does happiness come from having meaning in your life, or is happiness simply the joy of the journey?

That's a lot of questions, isn't it? And it's only the

beginning. Each question you try to answer brings to mind many more. Fortunately, this book will help you deal with these questions and guide you toward controlling that one-way door effectively to achieve the life you want to live and the kind of room you want to create.

First, you need to get control of that blasted door. Right now it's swinging open and shut on its own. People of all sorts are flooding in, and the squeaking is driving you crazy.

What can you do?

When you are ready to fully take charge of your door, you assign that duty to the imaginary person who becomes a part of your personality—your Doorman.

Your Doorman stands at the entrance—at the one-way door—and admits or bars those who want to enter. Your Doorman does this according to a set of criteria that you provide. Happy, creative, positive people? Go right on in. Negative, pessimistic, unhappy people? Thou shall not pass.

In order to determine who to let into your room, you need to make some important choices—and choices have consequences. What do I want to do with my life? Whom can I trust to do business with? How do I deal with the difficult people in my life? Whom should I marry? Where should I live? Where am I going?

The answers to these questions involve choices.

First, you'll need to identify your values—both the values you live now and your aspirational ones. Then, you'll need to know who's already in your room and how they affect the quality of your life. Knowing what you know now, would you choose to do business with Person A? Would you try to be a closer friend to Person B? Would you even let Person C approach the door? With a bit of introspection, you can learn to make different choices in the future. This reflection is part of training your Doorman to guard the door based on your values. We call this values-based decision making.

But it's not just about guarding entry into your room. Managing your room is also about handling people in your room and living the life you desire in your room. All of these things are important to understand in order to curate the room and the life that you want.

Here's one other thought that might help you visualize this fascinating room that is your life: your room is not yet full. Your room has no maximum capacity. (Remember, we said we paid off the fire marshal.) There's room for more people in it—people who can mentor you to achieve the life you want. The question for you is: Who do you want to attract into your room?

It's Never Too Late

People who come into your room bring their experiences, their values, and their philosophies with them; and these become, in ways both subtle and staggering, parts of your life. For better or for worse, they influence how you view yourself and the world, not only in your personal relationships but also in your business relationships. We've seen this particularly within professional networks like BNI (Business Network International), where people who come into a networking group can have a major impact on the success of that group. Just one wrong person can have a disastrous effect on an entire group.

If you're not careful, the impact people have in your life will not be the one you want. The wrong people can make your life unbearably chaotic. Have you ever felt your life was like this? That it would help if you could turn down the volume on the noise some people bring into your room? That maybe you're fearful to turn people away even when you think they might bring more disorder than help? Or you're scared or embarrassed to stop the toxic people you encounter at your door, so you let them into your room to avoid conflict, and they begin creating mass chaos.

Is your room already too full? Really loud? Full of drama? Boring? Holding angry people? Or worse yet—several of these things? Conversely, have you ever felt alone in an empty space? Lost without a roadmap? In need of friendship, advice, mentoring?

If any of this resonates with you, read on.

Chapter Three

DETERMINING YOUR VALUES

an you name your values, the handful of concepts,
beliefs, or aspirations in your life that you deem
most important?

The silence can be deafening when we ask that question.

Rarely can people list their top handful of values when
asked without advanced notice, yet knowing your values is
a critical component of making the concept of the room
work, because they govern entry into it.

In teaching the importance of values, we've frequently
witnessed the personal revelations people have had once
they take the time to sit down and actually think about their
values. Creating your list of values can be as straightforward
or as layered a process as you'd like. The goal—however
you achieve it—is for you to recognize, acknowledge, and

establish a defined set of objectives and explicit values by which you live. These values will allow you to make decisions about who gets past your Doorman and gains entry into your room.

Let's Get Real

We have learned from experience that not everyone wants to write a values inventory. If this sounds like you, we encourage you to keep an open mind.

First, you need to understand that *what consumes your time controls your mind.* What is consuming your time in your current experience of life? How do you feel about that? If you're not happy about what's consuming your time, there's good news: you can change that. This change begins with the values you manifest.

You see, we can't tell you what your values are, and we can't help you work on who's in your room until you have a better sense of the values you'll use to make decisions about who's in your room. So you need to do some work. We know: you probably don't want to do your homework. But behave yourself and focus for a few minutes. If you do, you'll begin to see changes in how you think about the people in your life, which will then lead to positive changes in your life. You can take as long or as little time as you want. You'll get through this, and then we can move on to the next

Your

section. Shut off the TV, put down your electronic devices, and work with us for a little while. If you want to control your room and your life, you need to work through your values. These next two chapters are important because they lay the groundwork for curating the room you desire. This won't hurt—we promise.

Your values can be current and they can be aspirational. Your aspirational values are values that you desire to achieve in life. Jerry Porras, Lane Professor Emeritus of Organizational Behavior and Change at the Stanford University Graduate School of Business, shares, "I don't believe in words anymore; I only believe in behaviors." To this end, we ask that, for maximum benefit, you recognize the values you *do* act on and live by and which ones you are *striving* for. Doing so will give you clarity as we teach you how to manage who's in your room later on in the book. For the purposes of this exercise, aspirational values are important but different. Your current values are the ones you act on, and your aspirational values are the ones you are striving for.

Identifying Your Values

Below is a "starter list" of possible values that may resonate with you. Values can be written as words, groups of words, or complete sentences, as we'll show you later in this chapter. The following list is simply to get you to start thinking about what your values may be. *Feel free to mark the ones that reso-nate with you* and add any others that apply to you.

Values Starter List:

Achievement
Adventure
Authenticity
Commitment
Conscientiousness
Courage
Drive
Endurance
Family
Financial gain
Forgiveness
Friendship
Giving
Gratitude
Growth
Health
Humility
Independence
Integrity
Justice
Leadership

Lifelong learning
Loyalty
Making a difference
Mentoring
Partnership
Perseverance
Physical well-being
Responsibility
Relationships
Security
Service
Spirituality
Spontaneity
Success
Synergy
Teamwork
Travel
Wisdom

For a more complete list of values, go to
www.WIYRtheBook.com/downloads.

Interpret their meanings however you like. The point
is to review the list of terms and thoughtfully mark the ones
that resonate with you. You are seeking a body-and-soul,
heart-and-mind resonance here. There are no right answers
except those with which you feel authentically connected.

You don't need to complete this in one sitting. Give yourself the space to live with your responses and make revisions as things get progressively clearer to you.

People often benefit from using an elimination process when identifying their values. To do this, circle the top ten values on this partial list that resonate for you, and then slowly eliminate three or four of them in order to get to your more important values. Very simple.

To verify your answers, think about how you would be acting if a selected word or phrase really represented a core value of yours. Sentence completion can help immensely. Start off the sentence with "If this truly mattered to me, I would . . ." and go wherever it leads you. Your final list likely will encompass terms that you actively live by and also strongly reflect the person you aspire to become.

Here are a few examples to get you thinking:

- If **financial gain** truly mattered to me, I would stop running up credit card debt from stuff I don't need and instead start fully contributing to my savings or retirement plan each year.

- If **public service** and **making a difference** truly mattered to me, I would stop talking about volunteering and instead choose a charity to volunteer with each week.

- If **responsibility** truly mattered to me, I would stop blaming others for my failures.

The above exercise might not be easy, but remember that you can't live your values if you don't acknowledge the points where you're not quite there yet.

Sometimes people have a difficult time being honest about what they truly value right now and what they would like to value in the future (i.e., their aspirational values). The reality is, your current values are where you are investing your time now, and your aspirational values (i.e., the values you would *like* to exhibit in your life) are what you want to manifest in your life. **If we were to follow you around with a video camera for a week, we would quickly learn what you truly value by what you actually prioritize in your life right now.** The question—if we did indeed follow you around for a week with our video camera—is: How often are you doing things completely out of alignment with your declared values?

Now is the time to take all the unproductive behaviors and values and replace them with new values that will create a more fulfilling life for you.

If you wish to do a comprehensive online values assessment, a good friend of ours, Dr. Tony Alessandra, has developed an online report that will help you start to get a good picture of the values (or what he calls motivators) that are important to you.

The Motivators Assessment identifies seven potential drivers of one's values, or motivation, which exist in everyone to varying levels. By taking detailed measurements of these seven key impulses, the Motivators Assessment is able to offer the practical applications and insight necessary to maximize performance and project outcomes.

You can get one of these comprehensive reports by going to this website:
https://tinyurl.com/Values-Motivators.

Linking Your Values to Your Life

After you've finalized your list, write a sentence or two after each describing how this value is important to you and how you express it through your behavior. It's helpful to think of the different areas of your life where your values come into play. For each value, you might write a sentence or two, or you can sort the descriptions according to how that value is part of a range of life categories, such as "professional values," "parenting values," "social life values," "family values," and "values on where to invest money." There really are no hard and fast rules.

Here is a sample list of personal values and descriptions:

- **Family**: My family is my personal foundation. I cherish my time with my spouse and family, and I look for opportunities to grow with them.

- **Relationships and Teamwork**: I seek opportunities to grow and nurture strong, loving relationships with quality individuals, and I know I will get farther when I foster teamwork.

- **Leadership/Mentoring/Coaching**: I believe leadership is one of the most important attributes of my success. I seek like-minded mentors, colleagues, and employees. I enjoy both opportunities to mentor and coach others as well as being mentored and coached myself.

- **Physical and Spiritual Well-being**: I maintain healthy practices including diet, exercise, meditation, and I avoid things that may damage my health or psyche.

- **Lifelong Learning:** I believe that learning doesn't end with school. Learning is something I want to be engaged in throughout my entire life.

Diving Deeper into Your Values

In some instances, it helps to also have a Personal Declaration Form. This is a document that details your values within a much richer context. It contains sections that break down your values into different categories of your life. There are many ways to categorize your life, but we like to use these seven: (1) business/career, (2) financial, (3) family, (4) health and well-being, (5) spiritual, (6) friends and social life, and (7) fun (i.e., where do you want to have fun in your life?). The document has room to explain your "purpose" in life, who you are in a single word, what your formula for success has been, what your legacy will be, what your long-term intentions are in those seven areas, what your goals are given those intentions, and any affirmations or motivational and inspirational quotes that you like.

If you would like to complete this more rigorous exercise, you can also find a template for this exercise at www. WIYRtheBook.com/downloads. You can complete this document over the course of the next several weeks or months. Be patient with yourself as you do these exercises, and take all the time you need.

If You're Struggling to Identify Your Values

It can be tempting to write down what you think your values should be, while being somewhat hazy about what they actually are. If this happens, it will create conflict for you down the road. An excellent way to avoid this trap is to think of the five people you most like spending time with. Take five sheets of paper and put each of their names on the top of a sheet. You can also find a template for this exercise at www.WIYRtheBook.com/downloads. Next, select seven to ten values that best describe each of your friends' core values. Now review the five sheets and look for the most commonly identified values and write them down. The goal here is to end up with a list of the top ten or fewer. You are now looking at your own core values.

If the list does not reflect who you want to be or become, then it's time to get busy. You are going to need a new circle of friends in your room—people who live in alignment with your values and what matters to you. Your life is a reflection of the five or six people that you spend the most time with. If your core group of friends is comprised of solid, hard-working, fulfilled people who rarely complain, odds are that you are this way; however, if your core group of friends are toxic people who drink heavily and have many broken relationships, then this is likely to be how your life is.

This may sound harsh. It's not. It's simply one of life's most important lessons. Hang in there with us, and we'll show you how to do this.

Identifying Your Deal-Breakers

This step is an important part of assessing your values. Everyone needs to have a deal-breaker list, your "don't even think about it" list. It is the list of values, behaviors, attributes, characteristics, projects, etcetera, that you just won't tolerate—period. Let your imagination run free with this exercise. Most people find it easy to think of a few deal-breakers right off the bat. (You probably have no shortage of examples!) Then it can take more time to distill your biggest deal-breakers down to a choice few. Again, take time with this exercise. It might help to reflect on the following questions:

• When was the last time you were really angry and frustrated? Why?

• What makes your life less fulfilling than you think it should be?

• What is the trait that you most deplore in others?

• What is it that you most dislike about certain behaviors?

• What do you regard as the lowest depth of misery?

• What do you find troubling about your friends?

After you have thought about the questions, write down your list of deal-breakers. This list can be constructed from your responses to the questions above and from another source: simply record behaviors you despise. Write down the behaviors or traits that, when you observe them, seem like nails running across a chalkboard. These dislikes could be things like lying, drama, gross exaggeration, irresponsibility, stubbornness, or one-upmanship. In other words, take a moment to list behaviors *you can't stand.*

Next, create a set of rules or attributes that will help you make better decisions in your life. We've created some examples to get the creativity flowing. You need to determine your own rules for people you want to let into your room and for your deal-breakers.

Examples of rules for the people that I will let into my room from this point forward:

- They must contribute an equal amount to the relationship.

- They must work in a field that has a positive impact in the world.

- They must be loyal and honest.

- They must be open-minded and have a sense of humor.

- Examples of deal-breakers for the people that I won't let into my room from this point forward:

- I will not tolerate anyone who is controlling or narcissistic.

- I will not tolerate anyone who is always late and forgetful.

- I will not tolerate anyone who complains all the time and acts needy.

- I will not tolerate anyone who introduces excess drama into my life.

As with the other exercises, time is your friend. You might start with long, disjointed lists. But if you revisit them, you'll likely be able to boil down your deal-breakers to just a handful of concepts.

Knowing Your Values, Controlling Your Life

Knowing your values and deal-breakers is empowering because it positions you to take more control over your life. Your moments of putting out fires will decrease and moments of enjoying life—and the people around you—will increase.

Several years ago, Stephanie, a close friend of Rick's, came to him about a family emergency. Stephanie was at the end of her rope. You see, Stephanie had four daughters, and the oldest one, who was eighteen years old at the time, had been in a deep, passionate, and turbulent relationship with a twenty-year-old drug dealer. This relationship had gone on for more than two years, and it was wreaking havoc on Stephanie's family and, more importantly, on her three younger daughters. Bonnie, Stephanie's oldest daughter, would go days without coming home and would occasionally rob her family of money and jewelry. Stephanie tried every conceivable option to save her daughter and her family.

Rick suggested to Stephanie that she teach her daughter values-based decision making and the Doorman principle. After Rick explained it, Stephanie sat down one morning with her daughter and framed out a list of values and what they meant. They talked about integrity, motherhood, health, honor, and relationships. She then asked her daughter to imagine allowing a Doorman to stand at the doorway to the room of her life. She asked her daughter to next imagine that this Doorman had the power to NOT let anyone or anything into the room of her life if it did not align with her newly stated values.

The entire "meeting" between Stephanie and her daughter took about thirty minutes.

Stephanie called Rick a couple of months later in tears. You see, Bonnie came down to breakfast one morning. Stephanie and her husband quietly sat there in shock as their daughter explained to them that she had broken up with her boyfriend and that she would never see him again.

When the parents asked why, their daughter said, "Simple: he really didn't align with my values."

Our questions for you are these: How much future destruction, drug use, jail time, etcetera, did this simple little thirty-minute exercise save Stephanie and her family? You may or may not have a situation this serious in your life, but how much will your future be impacted by applying the lessons in this book to your life?

We'd like you to imagine drawing a line in the sand of your life right now. From this point forward, imagine that every future decision you make, regarding who or what gets into the room of your life, is completely and wholly aligned with your newly stated values. Now imagine what your life will be like if you compound these very powerful decisions, one on top of the other, for the rest of your life.

But wait, there's more.

Chapter Four

Assessing Who's in Your Room

It's time to take stock. Now that you have identified your values, let's assess your room. We have learned that the more conscious you are of whom and what you are allowing into your life, the more you can do something about it.

Knowing who to let in—or not—is crucial because we must live with those we let in our rooms, forever. Whoever is in your room *right now* will at least hold a nominal place in it *forever.*

Recent research shows that memories aren't simply forgotten over time. In one study published in the journal *Neuron*, neurobiologist Jeffrey Johnson found that, even if study participants couldn't recall specific memories, their brains reacted in a way that showed the memories were still there. Some professionals make intriguing points about the duration and power of memories. In an interview with us for this book, Dr. Daniel Amen, the psychiatrist and neuroscientist we mentioned earlier, said that "memories can't simply be deleted. In fact, the emotions that go with those memories become anchored in your mind."

Your view of the world is shaped by the experiences you have with the people you've allowed into your room. You might remember the person who genuinely loves you, praises you, or skillfully mentors you. But you will also remember the boss who chided you.

You can't undo the past, but you *can* curate your room to build a better future. But before the curating process can begin, you need to know whom and what you're dealing with.

Identifying Who's in Your Room

At the start of the book we asked you to think a little bit about who's currently in your room. Now it's time to take a full inventory. As we asked earlier: Who's in, up close and personal, with you? Think about who you are happy to have in your room and who you'd like to evict if you could.

This is a personal process, but here is a list of categories of people we encourage you to think through as you assess your life. This is truly just a starting place to give you inspiration. Give some thought to just how many people are on this list and in your room. Don't just skim the list; think about the many people in your room who fit each category below, maybe even write them down.

- Family members

- Friends and acquaintances

- Neighbors/community members

- Business associates (e.g., partners, clients, vendors) and colleagues

- Members of organizations or groups you are a member of (spiritual, social, business, sports, etc.)

- Social media contacts

- Other "screen time" contacts, such as people you watch on TV (e.g., news) or follow (e.g., bloggers). Yes, even them because if they are in your head, you're allowing them in your room.

- Projects and routine obligations/commitments (and the people associated with them)

You can see how crowded your room really is when you think of everyone. Now ask yourself, based upon what you see so far: Would you have made different choices had you known that anybody who came into your room was going to be in it *forever*?

Some people shudder as they think of whom they have let in their rooms. Others are fairly pleased with their list, but then scratch their heads when they begin to wonder why in the world they accepted social media friend requests from people who bullied them in high school.

Questions to Ask

Now that you have an inventory of the people in your room as well as your list of values that you previously identified, you can start assessing the resonance each person brings to your room and your life.

Here are sample questions to get you thinking: Who brings in things that align with my values? Who brings me joy? Who offers me support? Who is happy for me when something good happens? Whom do I learn from and view as a teacher? Who brings out the best in me? When do I feel most alive, and whom am I with when that happens?

After thinking through those questions, write a sentence or two that explains why you value the person and then link those sentences to your values. This step gives you something to refer back to. After all, once someone is introduced into our lives, his or her memory is anchored in our mind forever. Now's a good time to write reasons why you have good associations with people in your room. Here are some potential examples of what we mean:

- **Family:** My **parents** love and support me unconditionally, and they have done so when I was a child and as an adult. They are always there for me, as I am for them, even if we don't always agree. (Values = family, close relationships)

- My **spouse** is my partner in life. S/he has been there with me through thick and thin, and we can always count on each other for a good laugh, a warm hug, or a shoulder to cry on. (Values = commitment, close relationships)

- **Friends:** My **running buddy** keeps me motivated and accountable to reach my fitness goals. (Values = fitness, friendship)

- **Community members:** My **neighbors** are good people who are there to lend a hand, and I find joy in helping them when they need it, too. (Values = community, friendship)

- **Work associates:** My **business colleagues** are trusted friends whom I support and also learn from. (Values = friendship, learning, adding value)

Next, ask yourself quite the opposite: Who brings in things that don't align with my values?

Itemize as specifically as you can your list of people who cause you the most pain and grief because they don't align with your stated values. These are people who are holding you back and that you must learn how to deal with. (We'll have more for you about this later.) Remember that it is far more onerous to deal with someone once he or she is in your life than it is to not allow that person into your life or business in the first place. Think of a time in your life when you've chosen what you believe represents a good opportunity but have brought people into your room who don't represent your values. You'll begin to notice how this "opportunity" has likely cost you time, energy, or money—and likely all three. Here's a sample list to get you thinking:

- **Friendship with [name of person]:** This friendship drains me because my friend only calls to complain or ask for a big favor. This friend will never listen to advice from me or anyone else. This violates my deal-breaker rule of not having anyone in my room who introduces drama into my life. Also, our phone calls take time away from family, which is one of my values.

- **Board membership:** I thought I wanted to be on this charity's board of directors, but the board's disorganization is driving me insane and we aren't accomplishing anything. Although I joined the board to add value, I'm unable to accomplish that goal; the resistance to change is much stronger than my will to fight for something that is taking time away from my personal life.

- **Three-quarters of my social media friends:** Rather than getting enjoyment from social media, I get frustrated because much of what I see posted from my contacts does not align with my values. Rather than feeling connected with distant friends and family I am deeply committed to, I feel disheartened.

Coming to Terms with Your Room

What did these exercises teach you? Hopefully, you've already had an "ah-ha" moment or two and realized that you can make some decisions to maximize the impact of values you aspire to and also to minimize the impact of values you deplore. Equipped with a Doorman who knows your values, you will be able to push some people farther back, into the shadows of the room, and also to pull others up close to you, where you never lose sight of them.

Your Doorman holds the key.

Chapter Five

TRAINING YOUR DOORMAN

Did you know that being stressed out activates biological systems, including inflammatory pathways, that can be harmful to us over the long haul? Interpersonal stressors are often the most significant stressors we experience in our daily lives. The last time you were angry, frustrated, or feeling "stressed out," it's likely that you could name a few people in your room who were involved with the state of your emotions and feelings.

A research project at UCLA looked at biomarkers in blood that point to rising levels of inflammation in the body. The research revealed that the mere act of socially competing with others, whether it's at work among colleagues or at home among roommates, could trigger higher levels of inflammation. This is especially the case when those interactions are laced with negativity or strain. We've known for some time that stressful, dissonant encounters can raise our blood pressure, but the fact that a housemate or friend can negatively impact our biology, right down to our immune system, is worth our attention. The take-away is that our rooms' occupants significantly impact our health and longevity, along with whether or not we are successful and happy in life.

It's difficult to overstate the importance of keeping good company. Robert Kegan, an American developmental psychologist and author who has spent his career studying how we evolve as people, has noted that who comes into your life may be the single greatest factor influencing what your life becomes. In *The Longevity Project*, Howard S. Friedman and Leslie R. Marin tracked what traits influenced a person's longevity and found that conscientiousness was what mattered most. Another crucial finding was that strong social networks matter—a lot—for a person's chance to live a long life.

Getting along is much more difficult with people who have different values than you. This is where the resonance and dissonance conversation from the first chapter comes in.

And yet, if you are like most people, the door to your room swings open wildly. No one monitors or takes stock of who enters your room, and there is certainly no list of qualifications for gaining admission. In this chapter, we'll look at how you can apply the rules you developed for the values and deal-breakers you identified in Chapter 3 to screen *new* people trying to enter your room. You'll likely see that some of these strategies can also be used to handle people *already* in your room, which we will discuss more fully in Chapter 6.

Are the People Trying to Enter Your Room Engines or Anchors?

Over the years, we've recognized there are positive and supportive people we really want to be around. They are solutions-focused in their approach to most problems and are almost always willing to talk through challenges with a positive end in mind. **These people are engines.** They help us to be our best selves, and they motivate us to drive forward in a positive way.

We've also noticed, as we're sure you have, there are people who complain as though it were an Olympic event. (For the record—it's not!) They tend to be negative, argumentative, and obsessed with problems without any realistic help with the solutions. **These people are anchors.** They hold us back and weigh us down.

Who do you surround yourself with: engines or anchors?

This is where your Doorman comes in. Your Doorman is looking for engines, people helping you go to the next level in your life. Your Doorman should forbid entrance to the anchors, people weighing you down with a plethora of issues, problems, and complaints.

Your Doorman needs to help you consciously decide whether someone will hold you back or drive you forward.

One funny thing to remember here is that no one thinks they're an anchor. No one! If asked, of course they'll tell you they are an engine; they just do *not* like the direction you are going, and that's why they come across the way they do. For the record, they're an anchor—with a motor attached.

Now let's talk about the Doorman's job to find people who behave like engines and forbid those who behave like anchors from entering.

Controlling Entry to Your Room

We recommend controlling entry to your room today so you can start benefiting immediately.

In other words, you need to train your Doorman.

How do you do this exactly? If your Doorman is just a fictitious person who acts as a metaphor to remind you that certain people cannot "enter," then how does this really happen? Easy: by carefully determining your values and applying them to your daily decision-making process, you will begin to understand the long-term implications of creating a life that matters. Once you've created your list of values and your deal-breakers, you can consider your Doorman officially hired. With that accomplished, it's simply a matter of living up to those lists and keeping them on the forefront of your mind every single day, with every values-based decision you make.

When you are in the mood to talk to yourself, you could talk to your Doorman. When you are ruminating on something, use your imagination to talk it over with your Doorman. What we are talking about is having a conscious conversation—in your head—about the things that you want your metaphorical doorman to be on the lookout for. When people ask something of you, take the time to discuss it with your Doorman. Take time to self-reflect on who's trying to gain entrance to your room, and make a decision to commit or decline only after you've done so.

Please understand, it is okay to say no. Steve Jobs, one of the most successful businessmen who has ever lived, once said, "Here at Apple, we are far more proud of the thousands of things we said no to than we are of the handful of things we said yes to." We believe that most of us have an addiction to "yes," as if allowing more things into your life will somehow make you more successful. The more people and things you add to your plate, the more you have to manage and navigate and the less you will accomplish.

It's okay to have your Doorman keep people on the porch and to keep the door closed. The question is: How do you do this gently?

Learning How to Say No

Learning how to control your door can be challenging for many people. But to optimize the quality of your life, you need to learn to say no to people who act like anchors and want to introduce things that don't align with your values. Screening entry to your room is critical. If you don't, then you run the risk of heading toward a lifetime membership of the "I wish I'd had the courage to live a life true to myself, not the life others expected of me" club.

Sometimes people come knocking at your door because they want something from you and you either don't want to work with them or that project doesn't resonate with you or your values. Other times, you may be dealing with people already in your room, and we feel this is an important aspect of our message.

Here are seven ways you and your Doorman can say no and not come across like a jerk (or worse):

- **If I say yes, I'm afraid I'd let you down.** A very effective way to tell someone no is to tell them you believe you'd let you down if you do what they are asking. It might be because you don't have the bandwidth, the knowledge, or the expertise to do what they are asking; but, in any case, you're not the person to help make this idea a success, and you don't want to disappoint them. This type of response not only gets you off the

hook but also affirms your work ethic and shows you
want the person and their project to succeed.

- **Know the difference between an opportunity and
  a distraction.** Recognizing this distinction begins by
  knowing your own personal or professional mission.
  If you know your purpose/expertise/mission, then you
  can say no when someone comes to you with something that is a distraction to that mission. This strategy
  can be particularly helpful for projects that perhaps
  interest you *in theory* but don't align with your goals
  and mission *in practice, right now.* One of the best ways
  to apply this concept is to use the technique below.

- **Refer them to someone more qualified.** When we
  say no to someone, we always try to refer them to
  someone who is more qualified or more suited to help
  that person. We also try to refer them to someone
  whose mission is more in alignment with their
  project. Just because you *can* do something doesn't
  necessarily mean you *should* if it's not truly your area
  of expertise.

- **I don't do that.** Sometimes the request and response
  can be very simple. For example, when someone tries
  to convince Ivan to have a piece of cake or pie, he
  simply says, "Thanks, but I don't eat processed sugar."

When they say something like, "Oh, just a bite," he has no problem telling them they should feel free to have his bite—because he doesn't eat sugar.

- **Don't Seinfeld it.** One of the really funny things on the old TV series *Seinfeld* was how the characters would go off on some crazy, complicated subterfuge or ruse and end up getting in more trouble than if they had just been candid to start with. Be polite, but be honest and direct.

- **Propose something else.** If you are unable to do something that you're being asked to do, offer them something else instead. If you are a restaurant owner, maybe you can't afford to cater that 5K charity race for free, but maybe you can afford to donate several gift certificates for the charity to raffle. By proposing something else, you can still build a relationship.

- **When you say it, mean it!** Be a broken record. Sometimes people don't take no for an answer. Try to be polite, smile, and repeat what you said before. Don't be surprised if you have to repeat yourself multiple times before people understand you meant what you said.

In each of the above scenarios, you can start by thanking the person for thinking of you before declining the request. There's no need to burn bridges.

No can also be a one-word sentence. Occasionally, we all encounter situations where we don't mind burning a bridge. To put it another way, the above responses allow for the door to stay closed but not locked. Each response keeps the opportunity open for you to, at some point, welcome the person or a similar project into your room, because you've been polite, honest, and helpful. But if you encounter a person with a project that would compromise your values, then a simple, firm *no* works well. You're not being rude; you're guarding entry into your room. We know a person who was asked if she would research, write, and edit a full Ph.D. dissertation, and she was also asked to coach the potential client on how to discuss and defend the dissertation to his dissertation committee. Knowing her values, she firmly said no and never heard from the person again, which suited her just fine.

We have one last crucial suggestion: try not to let yourself feel guilty for saying no. Although we love to say yes as often as possible, sometimes the opportunity cost of saying yes is too great. In these cases, try to be at peace with your decision to say no and realize you are protecting entry into your room. Say no and then move on knowing that you made the right decision for you.

An artist we know, Elizabeth "Libby" Sheele, struggled

with saying no until she took steps that transformed her life. Libby admitted to us that she had been addicted to saying yes because she loved being available to people. She found that by always being available to everyone—people already in her room and others trying to get in for the first time—her quality of life suffered. She told us, "When I didn't have a Doorman, my room was like the waiting area of an ER—I was always admitting one wreck after another!" For Libby, asking herself whether something is an opportunity or a distraction has proven particularly useful. She shared with us that since using the concept of the room, no person or project is automatically granted entrance.

Welcoming Mentors into Your Room

Can you recall a time when someone encouraged you? Gave you just the little extra boost you needed to complete a task or finish a race? Apply for that promotion? That person was a mentor, someone who helps you do something that matters to you. These people are engines in your life. Your Doorman needs to be on the lookout for mentors. Mentors add more that is helpful than just a teacher's knowledge; they have the ability to see you in ways you can't see yourself.

Just as much as you want to deny entry into your room to people and things that don't add value, you also want to make sure your door swings open to those that do.

We need to surround ourselves with people we can look up to and who can mentor us. We adhere to the idea that if you're always the smartest person in the room, then you're probably in the wrong rooms.

Your Doorman can pursue aspirational goals for you. You may not yet be the person you are striving to be, but you are aspiring to be that person. We can apply the Pareto Principle to people in your life and whom your Doorman should screen for. The Pareto Principle, named after economist Vilfredo Pareto, is also commonly known as the 80/20 rule, or the law of the vital few, and states that approximately eighty percent of effects come from twenty percent of causes. Business professionals are often well-versed in this principle, knowing that often eighty percent of sales comes from twenty percent of clients.

We suggest that eighty percent of positive effects in most people's lives (aside from internal motivation) can be traced back to twenty percent of the people in their rooms. So the question becomes: How can you focus on learning from that twenty percent who are likely your mentors? Even more importantly: How can you increase the number of mentors in your room?

First, create a two-column list. In the first column, write down everyone's name who is currently in your room who enhances the quality of your life. That can be your personal life, your professional life, your spiritual life—anything that matters to you. These people can be family members, friends, community members, business associates, coaches, colleagues, spiritual leaders, and so on. Don't neglect anyone who is a positive force in your life.

Next, in the second column, write at least one action you can take to strengthen each relationship. For family members, it might mean arranging more quality time together. If a spiritual leader is on your list, make it a priority to attend services more frequently if you are attending sporadically now. For business associates, perhaps you'll want to extend an invitation for a lunch meeting or a discussion over coffee. Ivan has written extensively on the value of building strong networks in business, so if this is a new and unfamiliar area to you, consider reading more on the value of business networking to cultivate these positive relationships. The steps you write don't have to be complicated or earth shattering. The point is, you want to create a concrete plan that will help you fortify the relationships you already have with mentors. Then pick up the phone, send the email, or attend the social gathering. Take steps today to strengthen your relationships with mentors by engaging them and, when appropriate, expressing the value they have in your life.

Put your Doorman to work to let mentors into your room. Then dedicate the time necessary to develop those relationships. The impact will have a compounding effect.

Now what?

Chapter Six

HANDLING PEOPLE ALREADY IN YOUR ROOM

Recognizing that people can never fully leave your room once they've entered can be unsettling. What do we do with all the people who don't align with our values?

And let's face it: What about family? And long-time friends? How do we handle *them*?

We're happy to address this elephant in the room by giving you clear, simple strategies—*because even when people are out of your life they remain in your head.*

Making Use of Your Room's Storage Space

After identifying your values and assessing who is already in your room, you're likely to have a list of people you would have banned from your room yesterday. These are the people who don't align with your values and experiences that you wish hadn't been allowed to enter. You would have no qualms about kicking them to the curb if you could.

Ivan's mother taught him how to deal with such an issue: "Well, we can't quite kick anyone to the curb, but we can box them up and put them on a shelf." That's right, box them up and put them out of sight. As the saying goes, "Out of sight, out of mind." And, just to be clear, we're talking about the shelf that you need to stand on top of a six-foot ladder to reach. This is not an easy-to-access shelf.

Mentally relegating these people to your storage space allows you to regain control over areas of your life that they may have controlled. Take those people and memories, put them in a storage box, and put it on a shelf. Don't let them continue to control your life. The intentionality of saying to yourself, "I'm no longer thinking about you," can be wonderfully freeing.

We also encourage you to thoughtfully reflect on the experiences and people you are putting in storage and try to learn from them. This thought process will allow you to then circle back to your Doorman to make sure no other similar people or experiences will enter your room.

Here are a few examples of people and the experiences related to them that you might box up—and learn from:

- **A social group:** I thought I'd enjoy joining this book group, but it's not been a valuable experience. Rather than learning from the experience, all I hear about is small-town gossip during our meetings. I'll politely quit the group and free up one night a week for someone from whom I can learn.

- **An employee:** I knew when I hired Joe that he would need mentoring, but I'm finding it frustrating to support him when it seems like he doesn't care. More than that, he's late to work consistently—a trait that falls into one of my deal-breakers. I'm going to let him go and make sure his replacement values punctuality and demonstrates ambition.

- **A boss:** I've been putting up with my boss's disorganization and rude remarks for three years, and the situation hasn't improved over time; it's only gotten worse. I'm going to see if I can switch departments. If that doesn't work, I'll plan my exit strategy from the company by researching my options, networking, and applying to new positions.

- **A grudge:** I resent that my ex has turned my children against me by telling them lies. I am going to move on from that resentment and instead take actions regularly to reconnect with my children to show them I care and love them.

- **Guilt:** (This is a big one.) Sometimes I let people in my room out of guilt. Once they are in, I continue to give them attention—out of guilt. Many times I tolerate people's behavior out of guilt. Guilt does not make for good relationships, and it creates a caustic room. I am not going to feel guilty because of someone else's "stuff."

- **Family-member syndrome.** They're family—what can I do? They may be family, and it's true I had no choice on whether they are in my room, but I'm not going to let them run amuck in my space any longer. So all of this sounds good, but how do you transition to putting them on a shelf?

Mastering the Art of Benign Neglect

We adhere to the basic concept of getting more of what you focus on. A really good friend of ours, Dr. Mark McKergow, says that "if all you focus on is the problem, you become an expert on the problem. But, if you focus on the solution, you become an expert on the solution." We wrote this book to help people find solutions to creating the rooms they want to live in. By working with your Doorman and clearly focusing on what you do want rather than what you don't, you will be creating your own luck and opportunities. To the extent that you're clear, and only to the extent that you're clear, what you want will show up in your life. As it does and you welcome it into your room, the elements of your existence that you'd rather be without will fade into the distant background as a result of your not paying them attention. We call this the benign neglect approach to room management.

Benign neglect takes many forms. It's any decision you make that allows a person in your room (or an activity associated with that person) to move toward the back, which in turn allows someone else to step a little bit closer to you. In other words, you're making room for people and experiences that add value and joy to your life. Often benign neglect is unintentional—perhaps a byproduct of not managing your room well and with purpose. Maybe you've accidentally let a friendship wane by not devoting any time to the relationship. But other times, benign neglect can be intentional and progressive—a direct result of managing your room purposefully. It can be a deliberate strategy. Here are some examples:

- Suggesting that instead of holding weekly in-person meetings with a colleague, you have virtual meetings every other week.

- Strictly limiting your consumption of news or social media to a set amount of time each day.

- Maintaining membership in an organization but no longer holding a leadership role.

- Speaking with a friend when she calls, but only initiating a call to her once a month.

- Opting out of "pub night" or "wine night" in favor of staying in with your spouse or partner.

- Telling someone no. (Refer to Chapter 5 for many strategies to say no without causing offense.)

- Not responding to phone calls or emails quite so quickly.

- Shifting your time and energy to other people and not being available as readily.

The bottom line here is that benign neglect works—even if you do it by accident. We're suggesting that, when appropriate, you do it by design. It can be progressive—meaning that you gradually move into benign neglect over time. It doesn't have to be overnight.

This new context for your life allows you to mentally

and emotionally move elements from the foreground to the background. Those troublesome people and events that have had starring roles in the story of your life become mere dots in the distance. For the truly troublesome people, they go in the box and on the shelf so you rarely even think of them. In this way, you create space for what you actually want featured in the foreground of your life.

Homeopathic Doses: Your Cure-All for Dealing with Difficult Loved Ones

We suspect you'd be lying if you said you don't have any loved ones whom you want to put on the highest shelf you could possibly reach—maybe even cut a hole in the ceiling and toss them in the rafters. These nuisances are often family members or long-time friends whom we love and don't actually want out of our lives completely.

Arielle Ford, a leading figure in the personal growth movement, told us in an interview the value of homeopathic doses for handling people in your room. A homeopathic dose is when you take the minutest drop of medicine to treat a problem. Ford recommends creating guidelines for dealing with people you love but who might not align with your values or are just generally difficult to be around, for whatever reason. These guidelines will help you create structure for interacting with them.

Your goal might be to see people and connect with them, but only rarely and for short periods of time. That way, you still maintain a relationship but you don't get "infected with drama or craziness," which Ford cautions against.

Ford encourages people to make small changes that have big effects. For instance, rather than calling someone two months in advance and telling them you'll be in town for a week, call them shortly before you arrive and ask them if they have time for a forty-five-minute get-together over tea—tomorrow. Likewise, when your drama-filled cousin gives you a call, tell her, "It's great to hear from you! I only have seven minutes. Let's catch up fast." Please note that you don't have to use these exact words, but you get the drift. Using your own words, the technique can be effective.

Alternately, if you want to catch up with some friends or family members, do so at a larger gathering where you can see them and talk but where they are not your sole focus for an extended time. Holiday parties, family or class reunions, or other annual get-togethers can be perfect places to continue relationships without getting sucked into drama.

These types of people are draining, so it's best to recognize that and plan accordingly. In other words, have a plan for managing these people so they don't elbow their way to the front of your room.

Setting Boundaries

To manage your room effectively, you need to establish boundaries on what behaviors you will or will not tolerate from other people. These behaviors will undoubtedly relate to the deal-breakers you developed in Chapter 3. By drawing such limitations, you will be clearer about the kind of behavior you expect from others. If you do not do this, it will be easy for you to become a pushover. Many people are unaware of other people's limits and will force their behaviors on you if you do not stand your ground.

When you set boundaries, you can use a strategy called behavioral disruption. Behavioral disruption starts with communication, not confrontation. Clear, open, honest, and direct communication is almost always the best way to address issues, and applying this to managing your room is no exception. With behavioral disruption, your goal is to disrupt the process that allows your deal-breakers to be violated. To do this, speak with the person about the issue and share what your response will be the next time one of your deal-breakers is broken. When the person crosses your boundaries, remove yourself.

Rick used to have mixed feelings every time he picked up the phone for his regularly scheduled calls with his mother because she would *always* start complaining—complaining so harshly that some people would consider it verbal assault. Finally, he decided he would tell his mother that he loved his regular calls with her but was really uncomfortable when she focused so much on this negativity. He said that, from now on, when she launched into one of these controversies he was going to politely let her know that he needed to go. He'd calmly say goodbye, and he would hang up. After doing just that two or three times in a row, it almost never happened again. Rick set boundaries and then adhered to them!

Managing the people who are already in your room can be less stressful than you may think. If you put a little thought into how you want to handle different types of situations, you'll be less likely to be caught off guard and inadvertently let someone else take control of your room. When you're able to handle the people in your room in a way that adds value to your life rather than creates obstacles or stress, you'll find you're on your path to a more fulfilling life.

Thinking through these kinds of situations in advance will truly help you. Often, when people are dealing with stressful interpersonal relationships and they haven't really thought through their responses, they can come across as sarcastic, angry, or unfeeling. It's natural to give these impressions when you react to situations you haven't really thought about. Train yourself and your Doorman in advance.

You don't have to subject yourself to drama anymore. This can be a life-changing experience. **If you do the work, trust the process.** You'll be glad you did. Bookmark this chapter. We're guessing you'll come back to this one from time to time for a refresher.

But your room can be even better!

Chapter Seven

LIVING IN YOUR ROOM

Up to this point, you've identified your values, both the ones you are already living and the ones you aspire to, and you've learned how to manage entry into your room and handle the people already in it. So, now, how do you live in your room?

If you're like most people, at some point in time—possibly even today—you've thought about having better balance in your life. In this crazy, hectic, technology-driven society, balance is an ever-present concern for many people.

Would you like to learn the secret to balance? Are you ready? Here it is:

Forget about balance; it's an illusion. "Balance" assumes that we spend an *equal* amount of time in all or most areas of our life. It is like the image of the scales of justice where everything is completely in balance and equal. The concept of balance implies that we must spend a certain portion of each week devoted in some equal measure to every item important in our life.

The problem with this is that most people can't actually achieve this on a regular basis. We tend to live such hectic, busy lives that it is incredibly difficult to fit it all in.

But there's good news. We suggest striving for **harmony**, not balance, as you live in your room. This is more than semantics—it is a different way of looking at life. While life can't be fully in balance, it is possible to create a life that is in harmony with your values and vision of who you are and what you want to do. Even the symbol for harmony (the yin yang) is out of balance if you look at each piece separately.

Psychologists and therapists largely agree that awareness is curative. In this vein, we believe you likely won't be able to have harmony in your room if you aren't aware of the people and activities that bring you deep satisfaction.

To bring harmony to your room, find a place where you can sit in silence for a while. Have a pen and paper handy. We suggest you do not use a computer for this, as there is something about the process of writing in your own hand that brings additional depth to the process. You may find it helpful to gently close your eyes and focus your awareness on the process of your breathing for a while. Then begin to review the moments throughout your life when you felt most alive.

Ask yourself:

- What am I doing when I feel most alive? Who am I with?

- When am I enjoying myself so much that I lose track of time?

- What do I look forward to doing the most?

- What makes me feel fulfilled and satisfied?

- When have I felt the proudest? Who was I with?

The goal here is simple: identify the people, activities, and projects in your life that make you feel alive, satisfied, or fulfilled.

To take this exercise a step farther, you can also write a paragraph about each activity that gives you a sense of aliveness. What does that look like? Describe each activity as vividly as possible, and take some time to think through what it would look like to experience each activity more fully—and more frequently. You might be surprised what you discover. As a friend of ours started managing her room, she realized that it wasn't fancy dates with business executives who took her on helicopter and plane rides to exotic places that made her feel most alive, but rather it was a deep and meaningful relationship with a firefighter who is now her husband. It wasn't about the glamour; it was about the relationship.

Next, strive to say yes to more of the people and things that bring you fulfillment and a sense of aliveness, and strive to say no to the people and things that add stress and conflict within your room. When you consciously design your room, it is much easier to live a life of harmony.

In addition to being intentional about who you let into your room, here are some actionable techniques that we've developed to help us—and you—live in a room full of harmony. The power of these simple strategies will change your room and your life, but you must take action to make them happen! Write them down and refer to them daily until they are a part of your routine.

- **Be here now.** These are three simple words that will make a huge difference in creating harmony in your life. ***Wherever you are, be there***. If you are at work, don't be thinking about the time you didn't spend with your family the night before or what you should be doing with your spouse or partner. When you are at home, don't be thinking about the work you have to do at the office. Wherever you are, be there fully and completely.

- **Manage your time creatively.** If you have a big project at work that has to be done ***and*** you want to spend time with the family in the evening, get creative. We know someone who wrote his first book while his family slept. He would spend time with them in the evenings and after everyone was asleep, he wrote and ultimately finished the book without taking any time away from his family. We know parents who are pros at switching from "parenting mode" to "work mode" the minute a child goes to take a nap. Be creative and inventive in finding ways that you can accomplish what you need to do yet still allow you to spend time with the precious people in your life who bring you harmony. And remember, many tasks and projects have a finite timeline. You won't always have to resort to this type of creativity unless you want to.

- **Integrate elements of your life.** For many years, Ivan spent a couple weeks or more working remotely from his lake house in the mountains. During that time, he worked his normal hours but also had quality time with his family in a vacation setting. Sometimes he would have his staff and management team up for short retreats and work days. It was a great way to integrate work life into a leisure environment. During the last week or so of his stay at the lake house, he exclusively spent time with the family and didn't think about work.

Note: we aren't saying you should work during all of your vacations. What we're suggesting is there may be times when it makes sense to consciously integrate activities so you can have more harmony in your room. Look for ways to combine elements of your life whenever possible and practical, and do it in a conscious way.

- **Practice "letting go" and "holding on."** Contrary to popular belief, we do not think it is possible to "have it all." Unfortunately, life involves making choices. Practice understanding what things to say no to and then letting go of them. (Refer back to Chapter 5 for tactics on saying no.) At the same time, think about the things that are truly important in your life and hold on to them with all your might.

- **Create margins.** Life for people in this day and age is crazy busy. People will take up every spare moment in your life if you let them, so it is important to create a life that has "margins." Build free time, family time, and personal time into the margins of your day-to-day existence. We know someone who has "wine o'clock" each evening with his wife, during which time they enjoy a glass of wine, sit on the porch, talk about their day, and watch nature. No matter what "it" is, if you don't schedule it, it won't happen. You won't make it to the gym if it's not in your calendar. You'll be happier when you create margins—we promise. Schedule time to relax.

- **Enforce boundaries.** We bet you don't enforce the boundaries you desire in life. Worse yet, we're almost certain that you don't often communicate those boundaries to others. You need your Doorman to communicate those boundaries to the people in your room and then guard them jealously. Don't make apologies for the boundaries, and don't get mad when people want to encroach upon them. Why? Because it is inevitable that people will encroach. Simply state your boundaries clearly and politely, and then stand firm. Go ahead, give it a try. Your Doorman has permission to create the room of your dreams.

- **Live in your flame, not your wax.** When you do things you hate to do, you are in your wax—meaning you are doing things that are sapping your energy. When you are doing things that you love with the people in your room, you are living in your flame. You are energized and excited. If you want harmony, strive to do things that are in your flame, not in your wax. Say yes to people and activities that make you feel alive, align with your values, and add harmony to your room.

- **Make space for virtual mentors.** You can't achieve harmony unless you are living your values or aspirational values. Virtual mentors in your room help you achieve those aspirational values. Even though physical mentors are outstanding, sometimes they are not enough. As proponents of lifelong learning, we believe a room full of harmony includes space for personal and professional development. Sometimes you really do have to look beyond who is already in your room, and the people waiting to get in, to seek out virtual mentors particularly related to your aspirational goals and values. A virtual mentor is anyone you learn from outside a face-to-face environment.

  They can be found in books, podcasts, blogs, and online courses, and on YouTube. We encourage you to take a moment to think about which of your values are aspirational, and then jot down a list of who or what you need, such as a certain type of knowledge or skills, to get closer to living a life that reflects those values. This process of reflection helps you identify the types of virtual mentors who will benefit you and allow you to achieve the life you want. Nothing can replace a real mentor in your room. However, virtual mentors can also aid in the intentional design of your room, and these mentors will impact you in ways you can't even imagine now.

This reflection is about understanding what you want to attract into your life. The Law of Attraction is powerful. However, *action* is part of the word *attraction*. Therefore, you must take action to attract harmony into your room.

Living in harmony inherently means freeing yourself from any guilt you might feel for choosing one activity over another or one person over another. Guilt is an obstacle to harmony. Box up your guilt and toss it up to the highest shelf in your room.

The concept of the room is really about going from the unconscious to the conscious process of decision-making—and we've given you a framework to reset your mindset, to consciously build the life you want that is full of harmony, instead of just letting it happen.

The truth is that when you are seventy years old, you are not going to wish you had spent more time doing things you didn't like or being with people you didn't enjoy spending time with. Rather than striving for the constantly out-of-reach balance, focus on creating harmony in your room. Be creative. Find ideas that work for you and the life you live. Make the time and be innovative. Balance may be illusive, but harmony is possible. Harmony is created where harmony is sought.

You are the curator of your room.

Chapter Eight

THE ROOM YOU DESIGN

The power of *Who's in Your Room?* and having a Doorman is that you can now focus your energy on bringing people and ideas into your room to support the future you desire.

The way you plan your room will help you live your life in a way that is more by design than by reaction. Charles Swindoll's words about attitude— "Life is ten percent what happens to me and ninety percent how I react to it"—ring true to us. Attitude impacts your life more than what happens to you. Rather than living a life in which you feel like you have no control and in which things happen to you, you can design your room so you'll have a better sense of control when things don't go as planned.

Who's in your room? is a simple yet transformative idea.

It's about asking yourself what's working in your life and what's not. Self-reflection questions help you determine both your lived and your aspirational values.

Stewart has worked on personal transformation almost all of his life, and he knows that people **can** transform their lives. But Stewart also knows that people often **don't** transform and improve their lives because they fail to take the necessary action.

All of what this book teaches is meaningless if you don't shift toward action. You can't make improvements through thought alone.

Let's review what we discussed and the actions you must take to transform your life.

The first lesson was to help you realize that once someone is in your life, they are in it forever. The door to your room is an "Enter Only" door. Will you see them every day? No, of course not. But do they shape your actions, thoughts, and beliefs moving forward? Yes, because no matter where they are physically they will always be in your head. While that might be an alarming thought to some, it underscores the importance of knowing your values and then living by them.

Our second lesson was all about your Doorman. This Doorman is your conscious and unconscious mind guarding the door to your life. The Doorman uses your values as a guide to admit or refuse entry into your room. The Doorman plays an important part in the future you choose to create. Get clear on how your Doorman can change your life.

Our third lesson had you identify your lived values and aspirational values. Understanding these values can help you and your Doorman assess who is currently in your life supporting those values—and who is just adding clutter and chaos. Values-based decision-making is key to understanding this. Thus, you have to get clear on your lived values, aspirational values, and deal-breakers in order to give your Doorman the guidance he needs to design the room of your dreams.

Our fourth lesson reinforced the notion that whoever is in your room is in there forever. Because of this notion, it's critical that you assess who is in your room so you can intentionally decide who should be in the foreground and who should be in the background (or boxed up on the shelf!), moving forward.

The fifth lesson helped you train your Doorman to screen new people who are trying to gain entry into your room. It taught you the difference between engines and anchors, and it showed you how to politely say no in many ways to people who don't align or resonate with your values. It also trained you and your Doorman to say yes to people who do align with your values and who can be mentors who help you achieve your aspirational values.

The sixth lesson provided you and your Doorman with insight into handling problem people who are already in your room and whom you don't know what to do with. It taught you how to box them up and relegate them to your room's storage space by engaging in benign neglect and interacting with them only in homeopathic doses. This lesson helps us all deal with family and friends, in particular, whom we might love dearly but who drive us nuts (that's the technical term).

And in our last lesson, we helped you and your Doorman take the idea of balance to the dumpster and embrace harmony instead as you live in your room. None of us can have it all, all of the time. But we can build a room full of harmony that fulfills and nurtures us to grow and achieve personal and professional wellness. This lesson gave you many ways to help achieve a room and a life full of harmony.

Each of these lessons rests on an underlying belief that you can be the architect of your room and your life.

As lifelong learners, we have also come to realize that this process—managing your room and aspiring to new values—is never complete. The more we learn from physical and virtual mentors, the more we are able to live a life we want. You're never done with this process.

***Who's in your room?* is more than a meme.** It's about the intentional design of your room and of your life. We can have the best of intentions in the design of our rooms, but unless we are in touch with our values and train our Doormen to screen according to those values, we will have a plan for a room that is left unmanaged and out of resonance.

So now you've planned what you want. But to really get the room—the life—that you want, you have to take action. Yes, it takes some work, but we know this to be true:

The quality of your life depends on the people in your life. When you design your room, you transform your life.

Now take control of your room and create the life you desire.

ABOUT THE AUTHORS

Ivan Misner, Ph.D.

Dr. Ivan Misner is the founder and chief visionary officer of BNI (Business Network International), the world's largest business networking organization. Founded in 1985, the organization now has over 8,500 chapters throughout every populated continent of the world. Last year alone, BNI generated 9.1 million referrals, resulting in 13.1 billion dollars' worth of business for its members.

Dr. Misner's Ph.D. is from the University of Southern California. He is a *New York Times* bestselling author who has written 22 books. He is also a columnist for Entrepreneur.com and has been a university professor as well as a member of the Board of Trustees for the University of La Verne.

Called the "Father of Modern Networking" by CNN and one of the "Top Networking Experts" by Forbes, Dr. Misner is considered to be one of the world's leading experts on business networking and has been a keynote speaker for major corporations and associations throughout the world. He has been featured in the *L.A. Times, The Wall Street Journal,* and *The New York Times,* as well as on numerous TV and radio shows, including *The Today Show* on NBC and programs on CNN and the BBC.

Among his many awards, he has been named Humanitarian of the Year by the American Red Cross and was recently the recipient of the John C. Maxwell Leadership Award. He is also proud to be the co-founder of the BNI Charitable Foundation. He and his wife, Elisabeth, are now empty nesters with three adult children. Oh, and in his spare time, he is also an amateur magician and a black belt in karate.

STEWART EMERY, L.H.D.

Stewart Emery co-authored the international bestseller *Success Built to Last.* He has a lifetime of experience as an entrepreneur, executive coach and leader, and is considered a thought leader of the Human Potential Movement. Stewart has served as Visiting Professor at the John F. Kennedy University School of Management and led programs at the Stanford Business School.

Over the last 15 years Stewart has led thousands of employees and hundreds of managers through Vision - Values - Strategy - Leadership initiatives based on research from the international bestsellers *Built to Last* (Collins and

Porras), *Good to Great* (Collins), and *Success Built to Last* (Porras, Emery, and Thompson). Stewart has led workshops, seminars, and delivered keynotes all over the world.

His bestselling book *Do You Matter?—How Great Design Will Make People Love Your Company* was released in September 2008. Coauthored with iconic designer Robert Brunner, who founded Apple's legendary Industrial Design Group and hired Jony Ive, it is considered a business book that does matter.

A wonderful storyteller with a great sense of humor, Stewart has appeared as a featured guest on television and radio talk shows. He has conducted coaching interviews with more than 12,000 people in the last three decades.

In the late '70s he was selected by the national media as one of the ten most influential people in the Human Potential Movement. He has been awarded a Doctor of Humane Letters degree by John F. Kennedy University in acknowledgment of his contributions.

Stewart's portfolio of passions includes aviation (he and his wife, Joan, are both instrument-rated pilots and fly a Beechcraft Bonanza), coffee, food, jazz, baroque music, travel, and technology. He and Joan live by the San Francisco Bay.

funds, has invested into more than 100 different companies over the years.

Rick is the founding and six-time chairman of the Gathering of Titans program. This event is an "entrepreneurs-only" event in its 14th year, held annually at MIT in Boston. He is a graduate of Rutgers University with a B.S. in engineering.

In the 41 years since he started his first business, Rick has learned that business growth and success are accelerated when a few key principles are applied. When Rick realized that less than 1% of companies implement these skills, he decided to create Business Finishing School (BFS). The BFS program, both online and in semi-annual live events, is designed to teach the 12 Foundational Principles of Business, which form the foundation of the program. He believes that virtually any individual or company can be put on the straightforward path to prosperity and exponential growth by learning to implement these principles. Rick resides in Dallas with his wife, Melissa, and their four children.

RICK SAPIO

Rick Sapio is a lifelong entrepreneur who started his first business, a bicycle repair shop, after the death of his father when he was just 13 years old. Since then, he has founded more than 20 companies. Rick is the seventh of nine children raised by a mother with serious, lifelong mental-health issues. He learned early in life that it's best to think positively about the cards one's been dealt—no matter how difficult those cards seem.

Since 1994, Rick has been the founder and CEO of Mutual Capital Alliance, Inc. (MCA), a financial holding company. MCA, both directly and through its affiliated